# OLD-FASHIONED
# FLOWERS
## in Ribbons and Threads

# OLD-FASHIONED FLOWERS
## in Ribbons and Threads

*Heather Joynes*

Kangaroo Press

## Acknowledgments

I would like to thank my husband Jack for his untiring help and patience while I was writing this book.

To Doris Waltho, my most grateful thanks for typing the manuscript.

Many thanks to DMC for supplying the threads used in the book and to Cotton-On Creations for silk ribbons.

DMC Embroidery threads can be obtained at all good embroidery shops.

Silk ribbons as used in this book can be obtained from Merrigang Cottage, PO Box 205, Beecroft NSW 2119.

First published in 1994 by Kangaroo Press Pty Ltd
3 Whitehall Road Kenthurst NSW 2156 Australia
P.O. Box 6125 Dural Delivery Centre NSW 2158
Typeset by G.T. Setters Pty Limited
Printed in Hong Kong through Colorcraft

ISBN 0 86417 566 3

# Contents

# Introduction

The popularity of old-fashioned flowers never wanes, and their charm and suitability for embroidery, particularly with ribbons, has inspired this book.

The ten flowers chosen are old favourites and none is difficult to work. With each flower I have included an illustration of one or several items showing how the motif can be used. The designs can be interchanged with most of the items illustrated, sometimes with a little adjustment.

The addition of stitchery in threads is an important part of the embroidery and enhances the richness of the ribbons with a different texture. I hope readers will be encouraged to work out their own versions of other old-fashioned flowers and use them on embroidery to grace their homes, clothes and gifts.

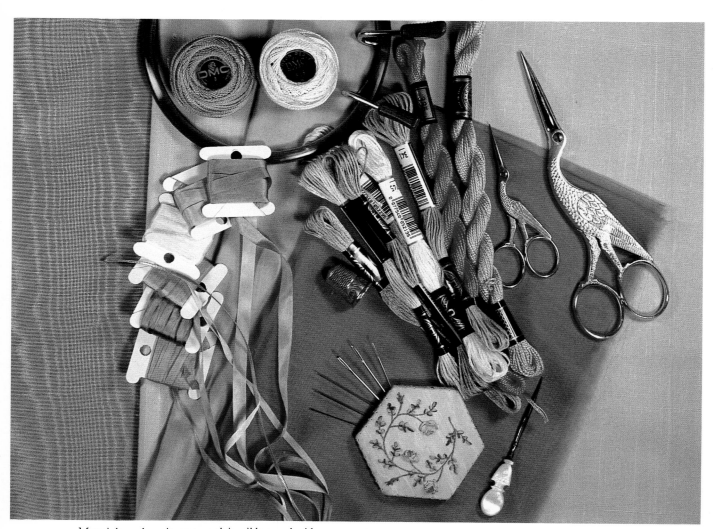

*Materials and equipment used in ribbon embroidery*

# Materials and Equipment

Fabric for ribbon embroidery should be firm. Velveteen, dress velvet, linen, polyester, cotton and silk are all suitable provided they are firmly woven. If using a fine silk back it with organza to give it more body.

The range of ribbons today is vast. Silk, polyester, velvet and rayon are available in lovely colours. Velvet ribbon needs careful thought as it is hard to pull through fabric and is best used stitched on top of the fabric if possible.

When buying ribbons without a specific purpose in mind 2 metres (yards) is a good quantity. Ribbons can be wound on the cardboard winders available for threads. This is the best way to keep them.

Tapestry and chenille needles in several sizes are essential, also crewel and straw needles in a variety of sizes.

There are many lovely embroidery threads available that will enhance ribbon embroidery. The most useful are stranded cotton, and perle cotton in numbers 5 and 8.

Other necessities are embroidery scissors and a larger pair, an embroidery hoop or frame, and a stiletto or awl.

# General Hints

When stitching with ribbon, thread the ribbon into the needle then pass the point of the needle through one end and pull taut.

Use short lengths of ribbon—about 20 cm (8 inches).

To start, pull the ribbon through the fabric from the back and leave an end of about 0.5 cm (¼ inch). When the embroidery is completed, sew the ends of ribbon down at the back of the work, using one strand of stranded cotton or sewing cotton.

Polyester satin ribbons need to be sewn down as soon as possible as they are very springy.

Anything that is worn or is to be washed should be sewn down very firmly.

If it is difficult to pull a ribbon through the fabric make a small hole with a stiletto or awl.

Do not leave long ends of ribbon or thread at the back of the work, as they are likely to get tangled and cause difficulties.

When pulling a ribbon through to the back of the work check to see that the needle is not piercing a ribbon already worked; if this happens it makes it difficult to pull the ribbon through and distorts the work.

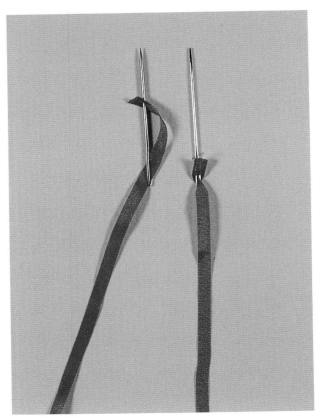

*Needle threaded with ribbon*

# Designing

The design must be suitable in scale for the article you are making. Always establish the size and shape of the article first, then the area to be embroidered, then the details of the design. Details of the design can be kept very simple, using just circles and ovals for flowers and leaves, for example.

Designing for clothing needs special care as the whole garment has to be considered as well as the person who will wear it. Cut an extra paper pattern and mark on it the area to be embroidered, then try it against the person it is intended for. Any adjustments can be made before working up the design for the embroidery.

If it is an important garment it is worth making a calico replica with the design marked on it. Time spent planning and designing is time well spent and will save hours of anguish and unpicking!

When working on anything with seams that will be under the embroidery, work on each piece of the article to within 3 cm (1 in) of the seam, sew up the seam, press on the wrong side then complete the embroidery over the seam.

# Transferring Designs

Only the bare essentials of the design need be transferred to the fabric to be embroidered. For small pieces, a dot for the centre of a flower and perhaps stem lines are all that is necessary. This is why it is important to work out the design first. It is not hard to follow a small design freehand.

For larger or more complicated designs, outline the design on paper in black felt pen, so that it is

*Design on net for transferring to fabric*

very clear. Tape this to a flat surface with adhesive tape. Lay a piece of nylon net over the design and attach it with adhesive tape. Go over the outline with a black marking pen, then remove the net and place in position on the fabric to be embroidered. Pin or baste securely in place. Now go over the design with a water-soluble marking pen or a sharp pencil. When you remove the net the outline of the design will appear on the fabric as a series of dots. These dots can be removed if they show after the embroidery is completed by holding a water-dampened cotton bud against them.

When transferring a design from a book by this method place a piece of firm clear plastic over the design before tracing it with a felt pen. This prevents the book being damaged by ink bleeding through the tracing paper.

## Finishing

Your finished ribbon embroidery can be pressed lightly on the wrong side into a well padded surface. A folded towel is ideal. Take care not to flatten the embroidery.

When mounting pictures make sure the mount is perfectly squared at the corners. If possible use acid-free board.

When working with glue, work over clean scrap paper—white is best, not newspaper. Change the paper at every stage of the construction.

A large darning needle is ideal for spreading glue and for applying a small spot of glue to a small area.

# Roses

*You will need*

3 shades 4 mm ribbon (allow 0.5 m of each shade for one rose)
    pinks 24, 26 and 8
4 mm green silk ribbon, shade 33
DMC Stranded Cotton:
    pink 957
    green 3363

To make a rose, take an 18 cm (7 in) length of the deepest pink ribbon, double it and gather it by whipping over the two edges on one side, then pulling up. Use one strand of the pink stranded cotton. Try to hold one end of the ribbon with two fingers while pulling up, to prevent the ribbon spiralling.

Fasten off, but do not cut the thread. Sew the gathered ribbon in a circle at the centre of the rose.

Repeat with the next shade of ribbon, sewing the gathered strip around the centre already worked.

Take a 25 cm (10 in) length of each of the medium and lightest pinks and thread both into a tapestry or chenille needle. Make long stitches around the rose, overlapping the stitches. Let the ribbon twist as it will, so that both colours are visible. Do not pull the stitches tight, but leave them a little loose.

Fasten off the ends of ribbon at the back of the work by sewing down with one strand of stranded cotton.

The stems are worked in stem stitch using one strand of green stranded cotton.

Each leaf is worked with a pair of straight stitches, almost one over the other.

The roses can be worked in other colours, in three close shades of the colour you prefer.

*Sample roses are worked on cotton/polyester*

*Opposite: Lingerie bag, sachet and pearl bag*

## Lingerie Bag (for hosiery, slippers or lingerie)

*You will need*
fabric 82 cm × 30 cm (32 in × 12 in) (the fabric
  in the illustration is polyester chiffon)
1 metre (1 yd) 4 mm silk ribbon in:
  pinks 24, 26 and 8
  green 32
DMC Stranded Cotton in:
  green 3363
  pink 957
2 m (2 yds) 1 cm (⅜'') satin ribbon to match fabric

Fold the fabric in half across the narrower width.
In the centre, 17 cm (6½ in) from the fold, mark
a dot for the centre of the central rose of the design.
   Mark the centres of the other roses and the centre
lines of the leaf sprays.
   Use a sharp pencil or water-soluble fabric
marking pen.
   Work the spray as in the instructions.

*To make up*
Press gently on the wrong side.
   Machine stitch the sides, right sides together,
leaving a 1.5 cm (¾ in) gap 20 cm (8 in) from each
edge.
   Fold the top edge over and baste a hem level with
the lower edge of the gap. Machine stitch the hem
and another row 1.5 cm (¾ in) above it.
   Turn right side out and press seams.
   Cut the satin ribbon in half and thread each piece
through the casing. If necessary trim the ends, then
tie a knot about 10 cm (4 in) from the ends.

## Handkerchief Sachet

*You will need*
2 pieces fabric 20 cm × 41 cm (8 in × 16 in) (the
  fabric in the illustration is polyester moiré)
2 metres (2 yds) each of 4 mm silk ribbon in:
  pinks 24, 26 and 8
  green 32
DMC Stranded Cotton in:
  green 3363
  pink 957
thin wadding 18 cm × 38 cm
1 metre (1 yd) 4 mm satin ribbon to match the fabric

Mark the centres of the roses on one end of fabric
and the centre lines of the sprays of leaves, making
sure the design is well centred.
   Using an embroidery hoop or frame, work the
design as in the instructions.

*To make up*
Remove the work from the frame and press gently
on the wrong side.
   Cut the wadding very carefully to size, with very
straight edges. Rule lines on the wadding to help
keep the lines straight.
   Fold the embroidered piece over the wadding and
baste, making the corners as neat and flat as possible.
It is advisable to cut away some of the fabric at the
corners, but be careful, as it is easy to cut away too
much.
   Turn under and pin the other piece of fabric to
the inside of the first piece, then ladder stitch together
(see page 53).
   The sachet is finished with two ribbon bows at
the front corners. Sew an 18 cm (7 in) length of satin
ribbon to each corner and tie in a bow.

## Pearl Bag

A small bag to keep precious pearls or other beads or jewellery makes a nice gift.

*You will need*
2 pieces of fabric 12 cm × 31 cm (5 in × 12 in)
  (the fabric in the illustration is silk)
0.5 m (½ yd) 4 mm silk ribbon in:
  pinks 24, 26 and 8
  green 32
DMC Stranded Cotton in:
  green 3363
  pink 957
1 metre (1 yd) 4 mm ribbon to match fabric

Mark the centre of the rose with a dot, and the centre line of the leaf sprays. Use a sharp pencil or water-soluble fabric marking pen. Work the spray as described.

*To make up*
Press gently on the wrong side.
  Machine the two pieces of fabric around three sides, right sides together, leaving one of the short ends open. Leave a 1 cm (¼ in) gap in the seam 5 cm (2 in) from each end of the long sides.
  Turn right side out and press the seams flat.
  Turn in open end 1 cm (¼ in) and slip stitch.
  Machine stitch two rows of straight stitching across each end at gap in side seams.
  The ends of the threads should be threaded into a needle and taken into the side seam for a neat finish.
  Fold the bag in half and ladder stitch the sides together below the casing (page 53).

*To make the drawstring*
Thread two 40 cm (16 in) lengths of ribbon through the casing in opposite directions so that the ends of the two ribbons come out on opposite sides of the casing. Make knots in the ends of each ribbon.

# Hollyhocks

*You will need*
1 metre (1 yd) 4 mm silk ribbon in:
  reds 92, 93, 69
DMC Stranded Cotton in:
  greens 3346, 3013, 523
  reds 326, 309
  pinks 956, 335
  yellow 745

Work the stems of the hollyhocks first, in whipped chain stitch in green 3346.

For the flowers, take 9 cm (3½ in) lengths of ribbon in reds 92 and 93, used together one over the other. Whip the edges of the ribbons together with one strand of stranded cotton and pull up, holding one end of the ribbons between two fingers to prevent spiralling. Gather to a 4.5 cm (2¾ in) length. Fasten securely, but do not cut the thread. Sew this gathered piece in a tight circle for the centre of the flower.

Repeat with another two 9 cm (3½ in) lengths of ribbon in reds 93 and 69, and sew this around

*Hollyhocks sample worked on linen/polyester*

the centre piece. Tuck the end under neatly and make sure the gathering is well anchored. Add more stitches if necessary. It is quite fiddly to do, but the effect is worth the effort.

The opening buds are short straight stitches in ribbon. Add two or three tiny chain stitches at the base of the bud, using one strand of green 3346. Stalks are in stem stitch in the same thread.

The unopened buds are French knots in eight strands of green 523 (use four strands doubled).

Seeds are straight stitches in two strands of green 3013.

The leaves are worked in fly stitch using three strands of green 3346 and working two fly stitches, one inside the other, for every point of the leaf.

Work veins in back stitch in one strand of the same green.

The single hollyhocks are worked in buttonhole stitch in two strands of pink 956, and sometimes 335. The buttonhole stitches are worked unevenly in groups, making a fan shape, with the edge of the stitch undulating. To start on a new fan shape, bring the needle up outside the previous shape and continue. From the centre of the flower work straight

*Tea cosy and traycloth*

stitches in two strands of red 326, making the stitches uneven and placing them between the buttonhole stitches.

Make a bullion knot in two strands of yellow 745 at the centre of the flower.

Opening buds are in chain stitch, worked one inside the other; for larger buds work three chain stitch pairs, for smaller ones one pair.

## Single Hollyhocks

These are worked in stitches only.

*You will need*
DMC Stranded Cotton in:
  pinks 956, 335
  reds 326, 309
  greens 3346, 3013, 523
  yellow 745

Start with the main stems, worked in whipped chain stitch using two strands of green 3346. Next work the flowers in buttonhole stitch, with two strands of pink. Make the back of the buttonhole stitch undulate, and the stitches uneven, working in fan-shaped blocks. Start a new block just behind the previous one.

Using two strands of red 326 work straight stitches of different lengths radiating from the centre of the flower.

A bullion knot in two strands of yellow finishes the flower.

Buds are composed of one, two or three small

detached chain stitches in two strands of red 326. Two or three small detached chains in one strand of green 3346 are worked at the sides of the bud.

Unopened buds, leaves and seeds are worked in the same way as in the ribbon flower spike.

## Tea Cosy

*You will need*
2 pieces fabric 40 cm × 30 cm (16 in × 12 in)
2 metres 4 mm silk ribbon in:
  reds 92, 93, 69
DMC Stranded Cotton in:
  pink 956
  reds 326, 309
  greens 3346, 3013, 523
  yellow 745

Mark the shape of the tea cosy on one piece of fabric, use a water-soluble fabric marking pen. Transfer the design to this piece of fabric using the method with net described on page 8.

Frame up into an embroidery frame, either rectangular or a circular hoop. The entire design should be within the frame.

Work the design as described.

When finished, remove from the frame and press carefully on the wrong side into a well padded surface.

*To make up*
Cut out both sides of the tea cosy to the measurements given.

Seam the rounded edges, right sides together, preferably with a sewing machine. Trim the seam and zigzag over the edge. Turn right side out and press the seam carefully. Turn up a 2 cm (¾ in) hem at the lower edge, and hem by hand.

On the right side work a line of whipped chain stitch over the hem line. Make a separate pad for the tea cosy from cotton and dacron wadding.

## Traycloth

*You will need*
Fabric 42 cm × 34 cm (16½ in × 13½ in)

Transfer three flower spikes of the design to the left side of the traycloth. Frame up into an embroidery frame.

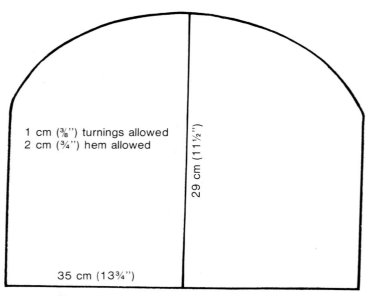

1 cm (⅜") turnings allowed
2 cm (¾") hem allowed
29 cm (11½")
35 cm (13¾")

*Tea cosy pattern*

Work all the hollyhocks in stitchery. This is preferable for this item as the ribbon flowers are very raised and would make a very uneven surface for anything to stand on.

Instead of the ribbon flowers work one spike in red 309, with the centres in red 326. Otherwise, work as before.

*To make up*
Remove from the frame and press carefully on the wrong side. Turn up a 2 cm (¾ in) hem, mitring the corners (see page 54). Hem by hand.

On the right side work a line of whipped chain stitch in green 3346 along the hemline.

Press again on the wrong side.

For the traycloth use the three centre flowers and appropriate leaves

# Heartsease and Violets

## Heartsease

*You will need*
4 mm silk ribbon in:
    purple 84
    yellow 12 and 14
    (allow 25 cm (10 in) of ribbon in each colour for
    every flower)
DMC Stranded Cotton in:
    green 3346
    brown 433

Start with the purple ribbon and make two pairs of straight stitches for the two petals at the top of the flower.

With the lighter yellow ribbon work the next petals in the same way.

Then work three straight stitches for the lower petal, using the deeper yellow ribbon. Keep the ribbon as flat as possible. The flowers can be varied a little by making the side petals in one stitch of each yellow.

Work two straight stitches in brown cotton (one strand) in each side petal and three in the lower petal.

Stems are long straight stitches in two strands of green, and the leaves are also worked in straight stitches, angling the stitches to the centre of the leaf.

## Violets

*You will need*
4 mm silk ribbon in:
    purple 177
DMC Stranded Cotton in:
    green 3345 and 3013
(allow 1 metre (1 yd) of ribbon for each group of
    flowers)

Violets are worked in the same way as Heartsease, with two straight stitches to each petal. The petals are a little longer, and arranged in a more open way.

A French knot in three strands of green 3013 is worked at the centre of the flower.

Stems are worked in stem stitch in two strands of green 3345, and leaves in back stitch in two strands of the same thread.

*Heartsease and violets sample worked on cotton/polyester*

## Large Lavender Bag

*You will need*
sheer fabric 80 cm × 15 cm (32 in × 6 in) (silk
    organza, chiffon, polyester chiffon are all suitable)
ribbons and threads for the flower motif (see page 18)
0.5 metre (½ yd) 4 mm satin ribbon in two colours
    to tone with the fabric and embroidery
dried lavender or potpourri

When working on sheer fabric take care to ensure that the back of the work is as neat as possible, and that there are no ribbon ends or threads showing through. Work each flower separately and finish off all ends of ribbon as neatly as possible.

Fold the ends of the piece of fabric to the centre and pin. Press the fold at each end.

*Heartsease and violets lavender sachets*

Trace the design onto one end of the fabric, about 10 cm (4 in) from the fold, using a sharp pencil or water-soluble fabric marking pen. Just make a dot for the centres of the flowers and only trace what is absolutely necessary.

Work the embroidery as in the instructions on page 18.

*To make up*
Fold the fabric in half, right sides together, and machine stitch each side.

Trim the seam and zigzag over the edge (zigzag 2, stitch length 1). Turn right side out and press.

Fill with dried lavender, leaving at least 5 cm (2 in) space at the folded edge. Gather and stitch securely 5 cm (2 in) from the top.

With the two lengths of ribbon tie a bow around the gathers and secure with a few stitches.

## Medium Lavender Bag

*You will need*
2 pieces sheer fabric 18 cm × 30 cm (7 in × 12 in)
silk ribbons and threads for the flower motif (see page18)
0.5 metre (½ yd) of 4 mm satin ribbon in two colours to tone with fabric and embroidery

*To make up*
Fold each piece of fabric in half, but do not cut out the shape.

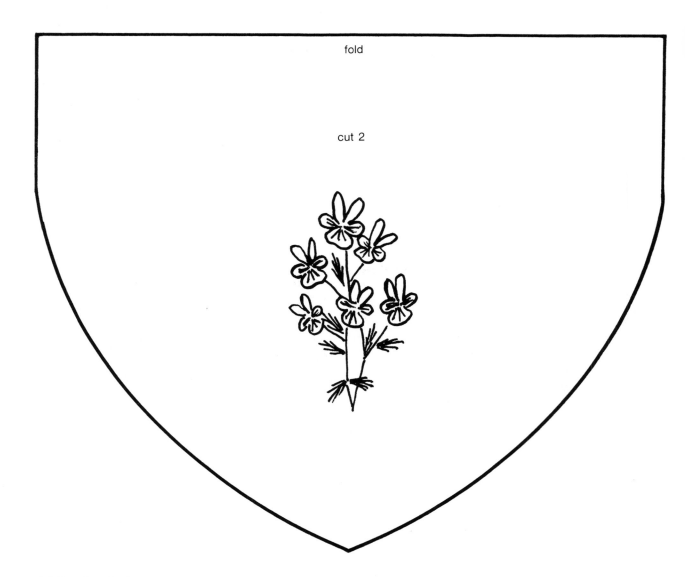

*Medium lavender bag pattern*

Trace the bare essentials onto one piece of folded fabric at the centre and towards the edge away from the fold.

Work the embroidery, then cut out the shape on each piece of fabric.

With right sides together machine stitch around the cut edges. Trim the seam and zigzag the edge (zigzag 2, stitch length 1). Turn right side out and press.

Fill with lavender or potpourri, leaving 4 cm (1½ in) space at the folded edge. Gather and sew securely 4 cm (1½ in) from the top.

Tie the ribbons in a bow around the gathers and secure with a few stitches.

## Heart-Shaped Lavender Bag

*You will need*
2 pieces sheer fabric 11 cm × 20 cm (4½ in × 8 in)
ribbons and threads for the flower motif (see
    page 18)
0.5 metre (½ yd) 8 mm (¼ in) satin ribbon to tone
    with the fabric and embroidery

*To make up*
Fold each piece of fabric at the centre of the 20 cm (8 in) side, and trace the motif onto the centre of one folded piece.

Work the embroidery as in the instructions on page 18.

Cut out a heart in paper using the diagram as a guide.

Put the two pieces of folded fabric right sides together. Baste the paper heart to the fabric with the straight edge at the fold. Machine stitch around the paper (not on the paper), leaving the folds unstitched. A small stitch is best.

Trim the seam and zigzag over the edge (zigzag 2, stitch length 1). Turn right side out and press the seam.

Fill with lavender, not too full, then sew up the opening with ladder stitch. Make a small pleat at the centre of the fold, across the heart, and sew down neatly. Fold the ribbon in half, and sew to the centre of the pleat 10 cm (4 in) from the fold. Tie a bow with the two ends of ribbon and secure with a few stitches.

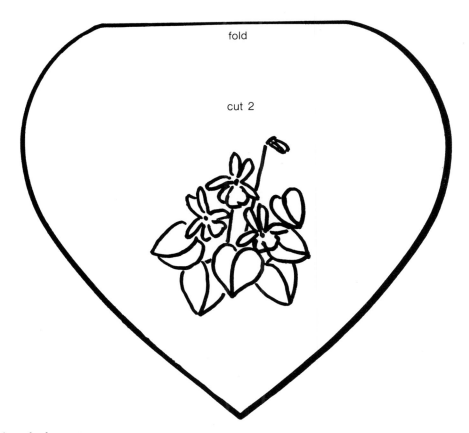

*Heart-shaped lavender bag pattern*

# English Daisies

*You will need*
2 mm white satin ribbon, 75 cm (30 in) for each
  daisy
DMC Stranded Cotton in:
  green 3347
  red 309
  pink 3731
  yellow 444

Mark circles with dots, using a sharp pencil or water-soluble fabric marking pen, on the fabric where the daisies are to be. A 2.5 cm (1 in) diameter is a good size. Mark also the lines of the stems and a small circle in the centres of the flowers.

For the daisies make straight stitches in the satin ribbon, almost 1 cm (⅜ in) long, leaving a small circle in the centre of the flower. Work pairs of stitches at N, S, E and W first, then fill in with more straight stitches. Some of the stitches will have to be a little behind the others. Always bring the ribbon up close to where it has gone in to avoid having too much ribbon at the back of the work.

Work small fly stitches in one strand of red at the tips of the petals, with an occasional group in pink. Take some of these stitches through the side of the satin ribbon. This will secure the petals in position.

Work the centres of the flowers in French knots

*English daisies sample worked on cotton*

*Opposite: Daisy chain design on a top, hatband and keyring*

22

using three strands of yellow. Work the outer edge of the centre first with French knots, then fill in.

The stems are worked in stem stitch with three strands of green.

The calyx of the profile daisy is worked with two fly stitches one inside the other, then filled in with straight stitches. Use two strands of green.

## Daisy Chain Hatband

The hatband is worked in a similar way on 4 cm (1½ in) petersham ribbon. Allow 1.5 metres (1½ yds) petersham ribbon and 5 metres (5 yds) white satin ribbon.

## Daisy Chain Top

*You will need*
6 m (6 yds) white satin ribbon

The daisy chain can be worked on a commercially made garment or on one that you make up yourself.

Choose a simple style in a firm fabric. Knits are not easy to work on and need backing with a suitable iron-on interfacing. The top illustrated is worked on dress linen.

Trace the design onto the fabric with a sharp pencil or water-soluble fabric marking pen, either from an already traced pattern on paper, or by the net method described on page 8.

Work the design as on page 22, starting at the back of the garment. If there are any discrepancies in the work, which sometimes happens when starting a new design or unfamiliar technique, they will be less obvious on the back.

If working on a garment to be made up, work the embroidery to within 4 cm (1½ in) of the shoulder seam. Then seam the shoulders and complete the design over the seam.

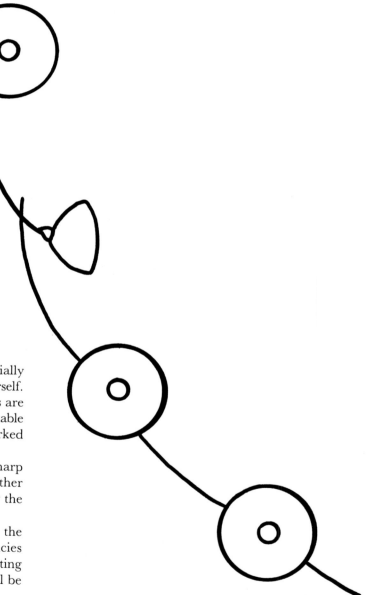

Front of daisy chain for top. Continue in similar fashion around the back

## Daisy Chain Keyring

The keyring is also worked on 4 cm petersham ribbon. A 20 cm (8 in) length is sufficient. Allow 30 cm (12 in) white satin ribbon.

Work the embroidery on one end of the ribbon.
  Cut a piece of strong plastic to the shape in the diagram.
  Make a shallow pleat at the centre of the length of ribbon and stitch down. Thread the key ring on the ribbon. Cut the ends of the ribbon to a rounded shape and run a gathering thread around the curve.

Gather one end over the plastic and the other end so that it will match. Sew the sides of the ribbon together with a tiny oversewing stitch.

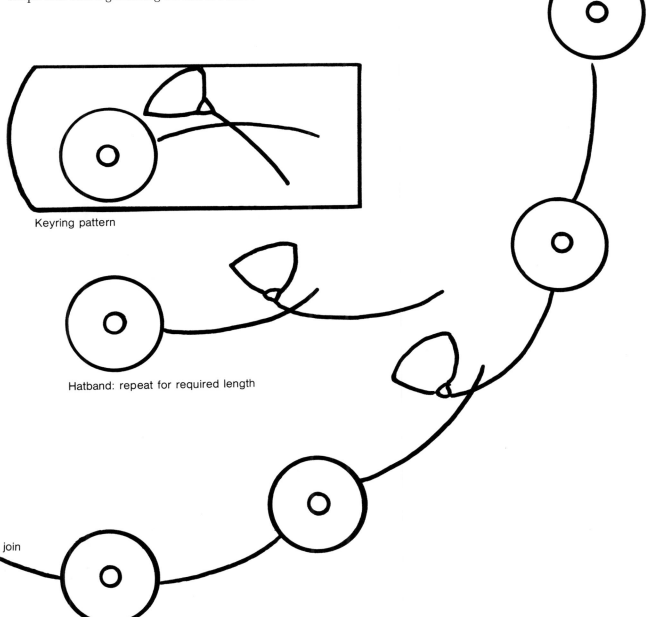

Keyring pattern

Hatband: repeat for required length

join

25

# Columbine

4 mm silk ribbon in:
  mauve 101
  yellow 13
  pink 163
DMC Stranded Cotton in:
  green 523

Start the flowers with three straight stitches in yellow ribbon. These stitches come in to a central point. Always bring the ribbon up on the outside and take it down into the centre.

From this point work three or four curls in the same colour. The curls are made by twisting the ribbon tightly and then pulling it gently through to the back until a curl forms at the tip. Use short lengths of ribbon, about 15 cm (6 in). The curls must be sewn down at the tip with one tiny stitch. Use a fine needle and one strand of matching cotton.

Work three straight stitches in mauve or pink over the first yellow ones, making them longer than the first stitches.

An occasional flower can be worked full face. Make five small straight stitches in yellow, then work five larger stitches in mauve or pink between them.

Buds are worked with two small straight stitches in yellow, one above the other, adding one or two stitches in mauve at the sides.

Stems are worked in stem stitch using one strand of green.

The leaves are formed with single chain stitches, each with a straight stitch within it. Work the chains in groups of three, varying the length of the stitches. Use two strands.

The groups should be close together to form fan shapes.

When working a group of flowers in mixed colours make one colour predominate. This will give a better effect.

*Columbine sample worked on polyester moiré*

*Opposite: Columbine cards and boxes*

# Columbine Cards

Precut cards for embroidery are readily available from embroidery and craft shops. Small pieces of fabric can be utilised to make these very special cards.

The cards illustrated are 11 cm × 15.5 cm (4½ in × 6 in) with an oval 10 cm (4 in) long.

Work the embroidery in colours of your choice as in the instructions on page 26.

*To make up*
Press the embroidery carefully on the wrong side.

Glue a piece of thin wadding, a little larger than the oval in the card, on the left-hand inside section of the card.

Glue the embroidery over the wadding, using very little glue outside the oval only. Be sure to centre the embroidery.

Apply glue to the section of the card with the cut-out, around the cut-out and around the edge. Press onto the section with the embroidery.

# Columbine Boxes

Wooden boxes with a recess in the lid, and cardboard box kits, can also be obtained from craft and embroidery shops.

For wooden box lids cut a piece of firm cardboard to fit loosely into the recess in the lid. (How loosely will depend on the thickness of the fabric being used to cover it. Velvet takes up a lot of space, silk very little.)

Cut a piece of fabric 2 cm (¾ in) larger all round than the cardboard and embroider the design on it.

Lightly glue a piece of thin wadding to the cardboard then cover with the embroidered fabric and glue to the back. Make the corners as neat as possible, cutting away surplus fabric.

The covered card should fit into the recess snugly and can be glued to the box.

# Geraniums

*You will need*
4 mm silk ribbon in:
    pink 103, 5
    (allow 2 metres of each colour for a complete design)
DMC Stranded Cotton in:
    green 3013, 3348

Each small flower is worked with five petals. Work two stitches to each petal, making the second stitch a little apart at the tip and into the same place at the base. Make more of the flowers in the deeper pink.

Make a French knot in the centre of the flower using three strands of green 3013.

Buds are a straight stitch with stem stitch stalks in one strand of green 3348.

The main stem is worked with two rows of stem stitch in one strand of green 3013.

The leaves are in buttonhole stitch using one strand of green 3348.

*Geraniums sample worked on linen*

*Opposite: Geraniums blouse and scarf*

## Blouse and Scarf

The geranium motif can be worked on a commercially made garment or one you will make up yourself. Choose a simple style, and make sure that the motif is placed well.

If working on a garment to be made up embroider the motif before seaming up the garment.

Follow the instructions for the embroidery on page 30.

For the scarf you will need a piece of fine fabric (silk, cotton voile, or fine cotton) 130 cm × 40 cm (50 in × 16 in). The scarf in the illustration was worked on cotton voile.

The design can be traced onto the centre of one end using a sharp pencil. Only mark the centres of the flowers, the stem and the outlines of the leaves.

When working the embroidery, keep the back as neat as possible, sewing down the ends of the ribbon so that they do not show through the fabric. Be careful not to carry over ribbons and threads for any distance as they will show through.

When finished, press carefully and fold, right sides together, and pin the seam. Mark the pointed ends with a pencil line, then seam, leaving an opening of about 10 cm (4 in) at the centre of the long side. Trim the seam, then turn the scarf right side out through the opening. Fold in the seam allowance and ladder stitch the opening. Press carefully.

# Delphiniums

7 mm (¼'') organdy ribbon in:
  dark blue 27
  mauve 37
4 mm silk ribbon in:
  blues 117, 118, 99
  mauve 37
  purple 84
  green 21
DMC Stranded Cotton in:
  blue 791
  greens 3013, 3346
Allow 1 metre (1 yd) of each coloured ribbon for
  a complete design.

The flower head is formed of loops, using an
organdy and a silk ribbon together in the needle,
with the organdy underneath. Keep a finger under
the two ribbons while pulling through, to keep the
ribbon from twisting. Use 20 cm (8 in) lengths of
ribbon.

Start at the base of the flower head using the
mauve organdy and the lightest blue silk ribbon.
Work three or four loops radiating from a central
position, then make a French knot through the
centre of the loops with a single thread each of
stranded cotton in blue and green 3013. Continue,
blending the colours, with the darkest colours at the
top of the flower head. Make several French knots
at the tip, using two strands of green 3013.

The leaves are worked in straight stitches in 4 mm
green ribbon, making the stitches in groups of
different lengths. A straight stitch in one strand of
green 3346 is placed down the centre of the ribbon
stitches.

## Workbag

This is a very useful workbag, as scissors, tape
measure, needlebook, reels of cotton, etc. can be
kept in the pockets on the outside, and thus are easily
found. Needlework and other necessities can be
stored inside the bag. The matching needlebook and
scissors sheath make a nice set.

*You will need*
60 cm × 110 cm (24 in × 42 in) fabric
  (the bag illustrated is made of polyester/cotton)
circle of firm cardboard 18 cm (7 in) in diameter
6 metres (6 yds) of 4 mm silk ribbon in:
  blues 117, 118, 99
  mauve 37
  green 21
4 metres (4 yds) of 4 mm organdy ribbon in:
  blue 791
  mauve 37
DMC Stranded Cotton in:
  blue 791
  greens 3013, 3346
1.6 metres (2 yds) 1 cm (½ in) satin ribbon to tone
  with the fabric

Cut two pieces of fabric 59 cm × 30 cm (23 in ×
12 in). One of these pieces is for the lining of the
workbag.

Cut one piece 59 cm × 30 cm (23¼ in × 12 in).
Fold this piece in half lengthwise and press so that
it measures 59 cm × 15 cm (23¼ in × 6 in).

Cut two circles 1 cm (½ in) larger than the
cardboard circle.

Divide the folded piece into six equal sections,
leaving a 1 cm (⅜ in) turning at the edges. Open
out and baste the divisions on one half.

With a sharp pencil or water-soluble fabric
marking pen rule three lines in each section for the
delphinium spikes and stems. Work the embroidery
in a frame, following the instructions on page 33.

When finished, fold the fabric in half again and
press on the wrong side into a well padded surface.

*To make up*
Place the embroidered piece onto one of the 58 cm
× 30 cm (23 in × 12 in) pieces with the lower edges
along one edge of the fabric. Pin together. Pin the
basted lines of each section, then machine sew.
Finish off at the folded edge by taking the threads
to the back and tying off. Make two 1.5 cm (¼ in)
buttonholes 6 cm (2⅜ in) from the top edge and
13 cm (5⅛ in) from each side.

Machine sew the other piece of fabric to the top edge of the piece with pockets with right sides together. Seam both the bag and lining, taking in 1 cm (⅜ in). Turn right side out, then fold the lining to the inside. Press the top edge. Turn in the lower edges of the bag and lining and slip stitch.

Make a casing 5 cm (2 in) from the top edge of the bag and 1.5 cm (¼ in) deep (the width of the buttonholes).

Gather a circle of fabric over the cardboard base. Gather the other circle so that the edge turns under 1 cm (¼ in), press, then slip stitch to the covered base. Put the base into the bottom of the bag and pin into the cardboard. Ladder stitch together.

It is better if the outside of the bag is a fraction loose, as the slack can be taken up when ladder stitching.

Cut two 80 cm (32 in) lengths of satin ribbon and thread through the casing with the ends on opposite sides. Knot the ribbon about 10 cm (4 in) from the ends.

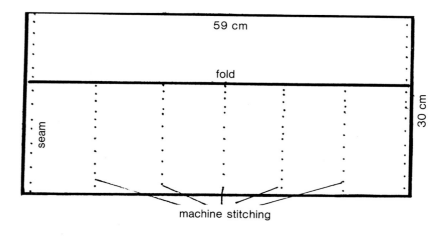

59 cm

fold

seam

30 cm

machine stitching

Layout for workbag

*Delphiniums sample worked on cotton/polyester*

*Opposite: Delphiniums workbag, needlebook and scissors sheath*

Scissors sheath pattern, actual size

# Needlebook

*You will need*
fabric 30 cm × 19 cm (12 in × 7½ in)
flannel or felt 14 cm × 13 cm (5½ in × 5 in),
    trimmed with pinking shears
ribbons and threads as in the instructions on
    page 33
2 pieces cardboard or thin plastic 8 cm × 14 cm
    (3⅛ in × 5½ in) (ice cream carton plastic is ideal)

Fold the fabric in half lengthwise so that it measures
15 cm × 19 cm (6 in × 7½ in). Fold across again
and press to mark folds.

On the right hand side of one end mark the centre
lines of the flower spikes and stems, using a sharp
pencil or water-soluble fabric marking pen.

Work the design as the instructions on page 33.

*To make up*
With right sides together fold the embroidered fabric
in half and seam the short sides, taking in 1 cm (⅜
in). Turn right side out and press the seams.

Turn in 1 cm (⅜ in) at the lower edge and press.

Place the flannel in the centre of the needlebook
and machine sew down the centre line.

Insert the two pieces of card or plastic into either
side of the needlebook and ladder stitch the lower
edges together.

A matching 4 mm ribbon can be tied around the
needlebook and a ribbon and bead tassel attached
to the top left corner. This makes a nice finish and
the tassel can be used to pull the needlebook out of
the pocket on the workbag.

# Scissors Sheath

*You will need*
3 pieces of fabric 1 cm (⅜ in) larger than the shape
    illustrated
2 pieces of card or plastic exactly the shape illustrated
fabric approximately 15 cm (6 in) square on which
    to work the embroidery
9 mm (⅜ in) satin ribbon 40 cm (16 in) long

Mark the shape of the scissors sheath on the fabric.
Work one spike of flowers within the shape.

*To make up*
Cover the two pieces of card or plastic with the
embroidered fabric and one of the other pieces. To
get a neat edge gather the curved edge around the
shape and lace the thread across the rest of the shape.
Turn the lower edge up neatly and sew in place.

Cover two pieces of thin wadding or flannelette
with the other two pieces of fabric, then slip stitch
neatly to the covered card or plastic pieces. The
curved top edges should match, but make the lining
at the sides and lower edge just inside the edge. Cut
the seam allowance plus a bit more from the lower
edge.

Sew the two pieces of the scissors sheath together
with small firm oversewing stitches. Leave the wide
rounded edge open.

Take the satin ribbon and couch it over the edges
of the scissors sheath. Start with the top back edge,
poking the end of the ribbon into the sheath. For
the rest, start at the lower edge, poking the end of
the ribbon into the sheath and finishing in the same
way.

# Honeysuckle

*You will need*
silk ribbon in:
    yellows 12 and 14
    green 71
organdy ribbon in:
    pink 11
DMC Stranded Cotton in:
    green 3347
    pink 758
    yellow 727
Allow 0.5 m (½ yd) of each colour for each spray.

Work the stem first in two strands of pink.

For the topmost flower take 20 cm (8 in) of the paler yellow and green silk ribbons and thread both into a tapestry or chenille needle. Make six long straight stitches, letting the ribbon twist. Leave the stitches fairly loose.

To achieve a curve in the unopened florets make a tiny stitch in one strand of yellow cotton to hold the curve.

With the darker yellow ribbon make two small straight stitches at the end of the longer stitches already worked.

With one strand of yellow work stamens in long-tailed knots from the centre of the floret.

Work the other flowers in the same way, but use the darker yellow ribbon and the pink organdy ribbon in one needle for some of the florets.

The leaves are worked in straight stitches with

*Honeysuckle sample worked on linen/polyester*

*Opposite: Honeysuckle picture frame and notebook cover*

38

*Designs for photoframe and notebook cover*

40

two strands of green. Start with a stitch down the centre of the leaf and then graduate the stitches on one side, coming to a point at the base, then work the other side of the leaf.

## Picture Frame

Ready-cut cardboard kits for frames can be bought at craft and embroidery shops. The honeysuckle design will fit a rectangular shape 25 cm × 18 cm (10 in × 7 in). To extend it (or make it smaller), alter the design at the centre of the longer sides.

*You will need*
cardboard frame
fabric 28 cm × 20 cm (11 in × 8 in) (the illustrated frame is worked on silk)
2 metres (2 yds) silk ribbons in the colours used on page 38
DCM Stranded Cotton in the colours used on page 38
thin wadding 25 cm × 18 cm (10 in × 7 in)
fabric glue

Work the embroidery in an embroidery frame, using the instructions on page 38. When finished press carefully on the wrong side into a well padded surface.

*To make up*
Cut the wadding to the shape of the picture frame and lightly glue to the cardboard at each corner.

Centre the embroidery over the padded frame and trim to 1.5 cm (½ in) around the edge. Pin the fabric onto the frame, pinning into the cardboard edge at the centre of all sides. Stretch the fabric as tightly as possible.

Place face down on a clean sheet of paper. If the frame has curves, cut into the fabric on the curves every 2 cm (¾ in) to within 2 mm (⅛ in) of the frame.

Put glue onto the edge of the frame, spreading it with a large darning needle, then fold the fabric over the frame, getting it as taut as possible. Work first on one side, then the opposite side.

Next cut the fabric out of the centre of frame, clipping the curves as before, and glue to the cardboard. The trick is to pull the fabric taut and not to use too much glue. Glue the back of the frame to the front around three sides only, leaving the lower edge unglued so that a picture can be inserted.

If it is going to be permanent it is really easier to attach the photograph or picture to the back of the frame with sticky tape before glueing the two halves of the frame together.

## Notebook Cover

Choose a firm fabric for the notebook cover. The cover in the illustration is worked on a polyester/linen, which is ideal.

Cut a piece of fabric the length of the notebook plus 3 cm (1¼ in) by the measurement from the inside front at the spine around the book to the inside back at the spine.

Work out the centre of the front cover on the fabric and draw the line of the stem of the honeysuckle on the fabric. Place dots for the centres of the flowers and ends of the leaves. Use a sharp pencil or water-soluble fabric marking pen.

Work the spray as in the instructions on page 38.

*To make up*
Press the cover lightly on the wrong side.

Satin stitch the short edges on the machine. This is best done with the fabric on typing paper.

Pin the front cover and inside front together over the book, keeping the fabric really taut. Remove from the book, mark where the pins are with chalk or fabric-marking pen, then machine stitch, right sides together. Turn right side out and press the seam, and the seam allowance for the rest of the cover.

Fit onto the book, stretching the fabric over the back and inside back. Pin together then ladder stitch into place.

# Lady's Ear Drops

*You will need*
4 mm silk ribbon in:
  red 48
  orange 88
DMC Stranded Cotton in:
  green 580
  brown 300

Work the main stem first in stem stitch, using one strand of green together with one strand of brown, and working two rows close together.

With red silk ribbon work the flowers in a long chain stitch, keeping the ribbon flat, and with a tail about 0.5 cm (⅜ in) long.

Work two straight stitches either side of the tail of the chain stitch, coming up away from the chain stitch and going down into the ribbon at the end of the chain.

The buds are worked in straight stitches, one in red and one in orange, almost on top of one another. Two small straight stitches are worked at the tip of the bud in the orange ribbon.

Next work the flower stems in stem stitch with one strand each of green and brown. Start at the end of the main stem and work the stem stitch right up to the flower or bud. Add a chain stitch around the last stitch.

The leaves are also worked in stem stitch, some in two strands of green and some in one strand each of green and brown.

*Lady's ear drops sample worked on linen*

*Opposite: Lady's ear drops tote bag and spectacle case*

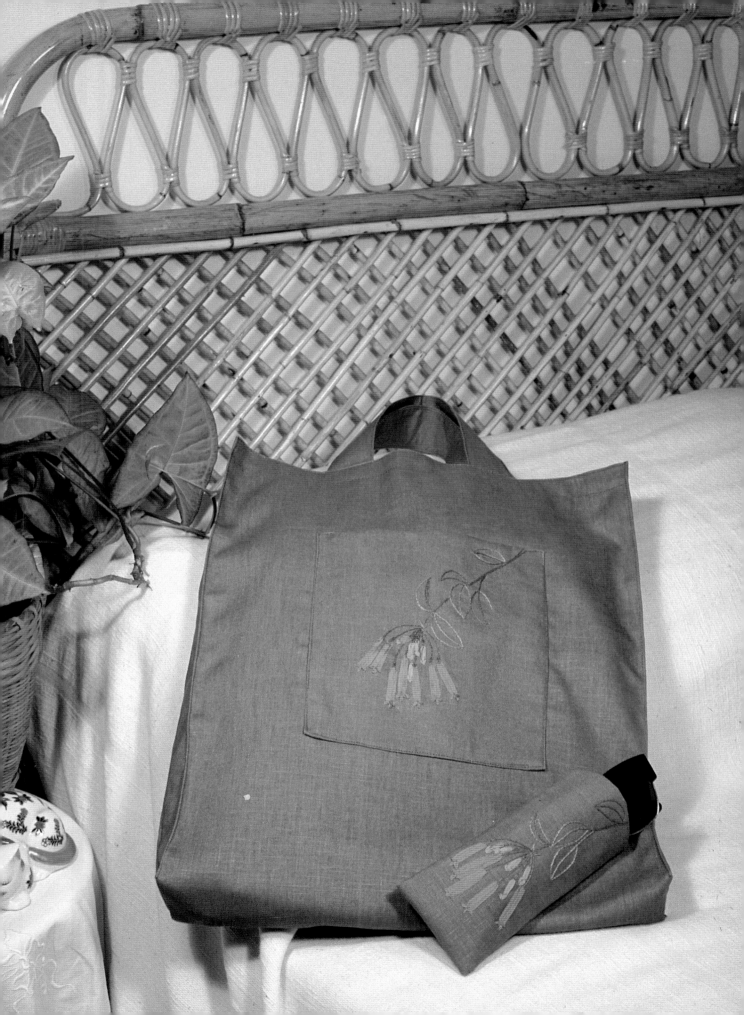

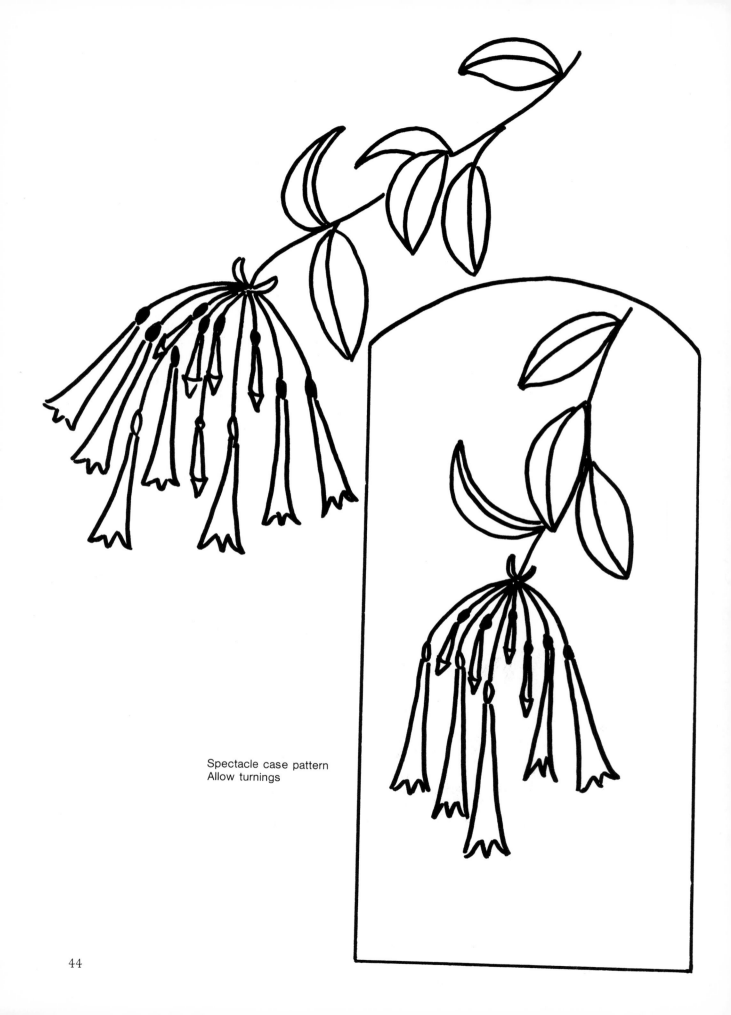

Spectacle case pattern
Allow turnings

## Tote Bag

*You will need*
1 metre (1½ yds) 115 cm fabric (the fabric used in
    the illustration is linen/polyester)
ribbons and threads as in the instructions on page 42

Cut out the fabric as in the layout.
    Transfer the design to one half of the pocket and
work the embroidery

*To make up*
Sew up the side seams of the pocket, tapering the
seams 0.5 cm (⅜ in) toward the bottom edge. Turn
and press.
    Pin the pocket in place on the bag, making the
side seams straight. This will make the pocket fuller
at the top.
    Press over the seam allowance on the handle, then
fold in half and press. Stitch both edges and add
two rows of stitching between. Pin the handles to
the right side of the top of the bag, with the top of
the handles towards the centre of the bag. Leave
2 cm (¾ in) extended over the top edge. Stitch
across the handles to secure.
    Stitch the top edges of the lining to the bag, turn
and press.
    Stitch the sides together on the right side. Trim
seam and zigzag over the edge. Turn and press.
Stitch seam on the inside of the bag.
    From the inside, fold the lower corners to a
triangle and stitch across the base of the triangle
2 cm (¾ in) on each side of the side seam. Turn
the points of the triangles to the centre of the bag
and handstitch down. Turn to the right side and
press seams.
    Stitch across the top edge of the bag 2.5 cm (1 in)
in from the edge.
    Edge stitch the sides of the bag to define the
gusset.
    Cut a piece of firm cardboard 0.5 cm (¼ in)
smaller all round than the bottom of the bag. Cover
with fabric. This gives a good firm base to the bag
and can be removed when the bag is washed.

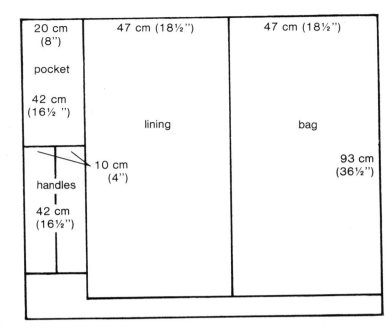

1.5 cm (½") seams allowed on sides
1 cm (⅜") turnings allowed on all other pieces
Cutting layout for tote bag, 115 cm (45") wide fabric

## Spectacle Case

*You will need*
2 pieces fabric cut to pattern (allowing 1 cm (⅜ in)
    turnings) with the lower edge on a fold
1 piece interfacing cut to pattern (no turnings)
1 piece thin wadding cut to pattern (no turnings)

Transfer the design to one piece of fabric. Work
embroidery as in the instructions on page 42.

*To make up*
Press lightly on the wrong side.
    Place the interfacing and wadding on the wrong
side of the embroidered piece.
    With right sides together, join the two pieces of
the case, leaving an opening about 8 cm (3 in) in
the centre of one side.
    Trim the seam, trimming the interfacing and
wadding as near the seam as possible.
    Turn right side out and press.
    Fold the case in half and oversew the sides with
matching cotton. Take in the inside of the seam only.

# Forget-me-not and Sweet Alice

## Forget-me-not

*You will need*
4 mm silk ribbon in:
    blue 98
    mauve 101
DMC Stranded Cotton in:
    green 523
    yellow 726

For each flower work five small straight stitches in a circle, making them mostly blue, with occasionally one petal in mauve.

The centres are in two strands of yellow cotton, worked in two tiny back stitches.

Stems and leaves are in stem stitch, using one strand of green.

## Sweet Alice

*You will need*
2 mm silk ribbon in:
    white 1
DMC Stranded Cotton in:
    green 3364

Each small flower is composed of four very small straight stitches in ribbon with a French knot in the centre in two strands of green cotton.

Stems are worked in stem stitch, and leaves in chain stitches, both with two strands. Seeds are a long straight stitch, with a small one at the tip, using one strand of the same green.

*Forget-me-not and Sweet Alice sample worked on polyester/cotton*

*Opposite: Forget-me-not and Sweet Alice cushion*

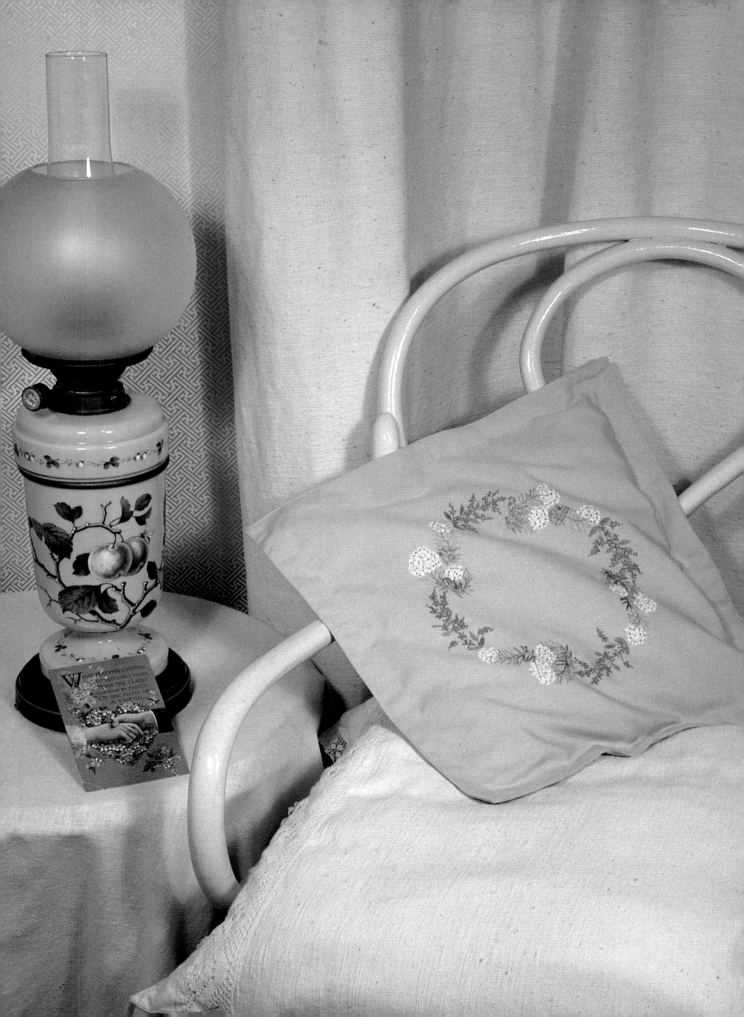

# Cushion

*You will need*
4 mm silk ribbons in:
    white 1—8 metres (8 yds)
    blue 98—6 metres (6 yds)
    mauve 101—2 metres (2 yds)
DMC Stranded Cotton in:
    greens 522, 3364
    yellow 726
0.5 metre (½ yd) 115 cm (45 in) fabric (the cushion
    illustrated is worked on a linen/polyester dress
    fabric)
35 cm (14 in) zip fastener
sewing cotton to match the fabric

With a water-soluble fabric marking pen mark a
19 cm (7½ in) diameter circle in the centre of a
43 cm (17 in) square of fabric.

On each quarter of the circle mark the main lines
of the flowers and the stems. Do not mark each floret
and leaf. It is quite easy to work from the diagram
once the main lines of the design are marked.

Work the embroidery as in the instructions on
page 46.

*To make up*
Press carefully on the wrong side.

Cut two pieces of fabric 43 cm × 23 cm (17 in
× 9 in). Sew the zip into these two pieces so that
you have a piece of fabric 43 cm (17 in) square with
a zip in the centre.

Open the zip.

With right sides together sew the embroidered half
of the cushion cover to the zippered back. Turn right
sides out and press the seam.

Add a row of stitching 3 cm (1¼ in) from the
edge.

*One-quarter of the design for the wreath. Repeat 3 more times around
a 19 cm (7½ ") diameter circle*

# Old-Fashioned Garden

This picture is reminiscent of the embroidery of the 1920s and 1930s when garden scenes in stitchery were very fashionable, awash with hollyhocks, roses, delphiniums and many other cottage favourites.

The flowers in the picture are on a smaller scale than their counterparts in the rest of the book. For the hollyhocks about 5 cm (2 in) of 4 mm silk ribbon was used for each bloom. The delphiniums still

consist of loops in 4 mm ribbon, but using single ribbons and smaller loops. Otherwise these two flowers are worked in the same way as the others in the book.

The roses are in two shades of 4 mm silk ribbon threaded in the needle together and brought through the fabric in a loop, tied down with several French knots in two strands of stranded cotton.

The smaller heads of flowers in the foreground are composed of straight stitches in 4 mm ribbon, in varying lengths, longer for irises, small for geraniums. Others are clusters of French knots in either two or three strands of stranded cotton, or tiny cross-stitches in one strand.

Leaves are worked in buttonhole, fly, straight and detached chain stitches in two strands of stranded cotton.

The picture is mounted on an arch shape cut out of firm cardboad. The shape must be drawn accurately on the board and cut with a craft knife. The embroidery is stretched over the shape and glued to the back with a good fabric glue.

An arch-shaped velvet mount was made in a similar way with a layer of thin wadding glued to the cardboard. Clip the curves in the velvet before glueing to the back of the mount, which is then glued over the mounted embroidery. A piece of matching fabric is stitched over the back of the whole mount, with small curtain rings sewn to it so that the picture can be hung.

If an arch-shaped mount seems too difficult the picture can be mounted as a conventional rectangle and framed.

# Stitches

## Back Stitch

Back stitch is useful for outlining leaves as shown, and for stems.

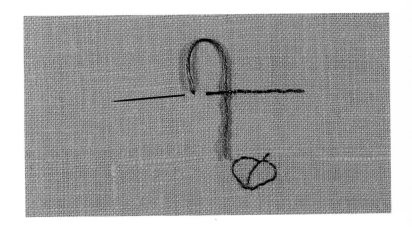

## Bullion Knot

Make a stitch as shown with the eye of the needle almost into the fabric. Wind the thread around the needle several times until the twists will cover the length of the stitch.

Pull the needle and thread through the twists, holding the twists firmly with one hand.

Take the needle down as shown.

Bullion knots make good flower stamens.

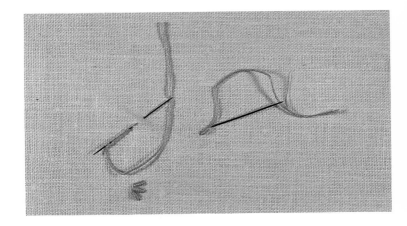

## Buttonhole Stitch

Make a stitch as illustrated, with the thread looped under the needle. This stitch can be varied by spacing the stitches or making uneven stitches as shown.

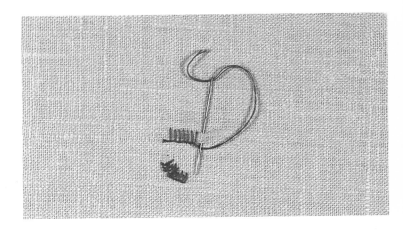

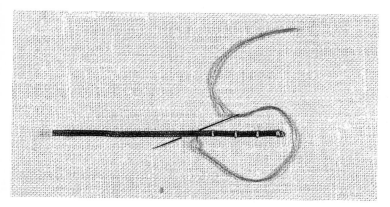

## Couching

Lay a piece of ribbon along the line to be covered and, with a thread, tie it down with a small stitch at intervals.

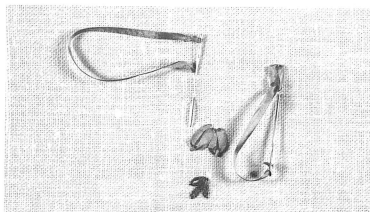

## Detached Chain

A most useful stitch for flower petals, buds and leaves.

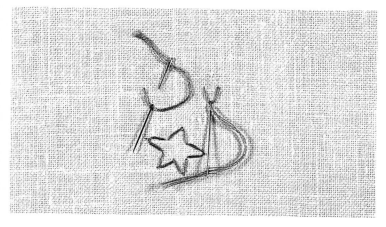

## Fly Stitch

This is a most versatile stitch and can be worked with long or short tails, in groups, horizontally or vertically.

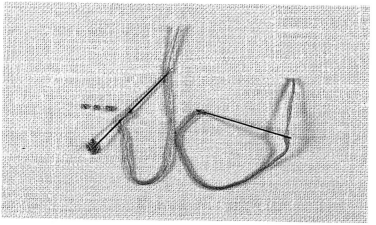

## French Knot

Bring the thread or ribbon through to the front of the work, twist it once only around the needle, pull snug, then insert the needle into the fabric close to the starting point and pull through to the back. Hold the thread firmly with the thumb while pulling through. French knots in ribbon need to be a little looser than in thread.

## Stem Stitch

Unbeatable for stems, whether thick or fine. Also useful for outlining leaves.

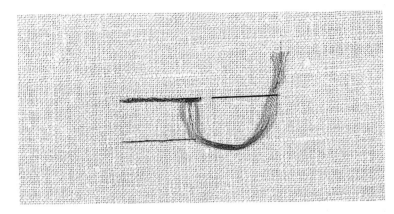

## Straight Stitch

Used frequently in ribbon for flowers and leaves. The length of the stitch is the vital point.

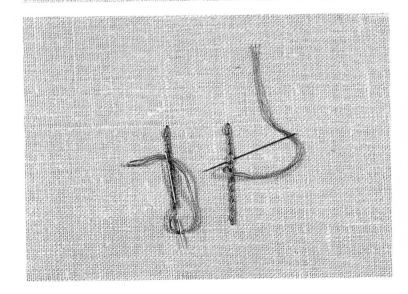

## Whipped Chain Stitch

This stitch makes a very firm, slightly corded line, very good for strong stems.

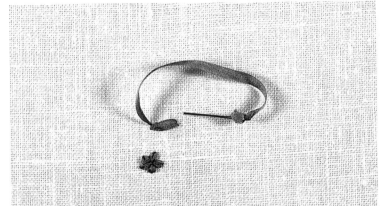

## Ladder Stitch

This is an excellent method of stitching two edges together on the right side.

Pick up the fold in the seam line with the needle, bring the needle and thread through and pick up the fold of the other side. Continue in this way, making the stitches at right angles to the folds and drawing them up so that the two folded edges are joined invisibly.

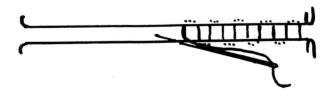

# Mitring a Corner

1. Press the hem allowance on all sides of the item. At each corner, cut diagonally across the corner 0.5 cm (⅜ in) above the point of the corner.

2. Press the diagonal edge over 0.5 cm (⅜ in), then turn the hem and press.

3. Bring the folded edges together to form a corner and ladder stitch together.

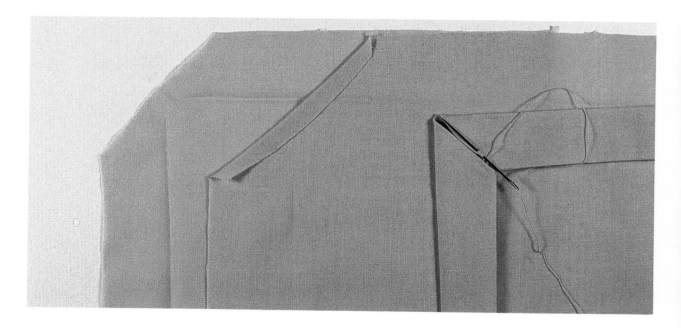

# Using Embroidery

Ribbon embroidery can be applied to the following:

| | | | |
|---|---|---|---|
| Bags | Coathangers | Handkerchief sachets | Pincushions |
| Bookcovers | Combcases | Hatbands | Sachets |
| Boxes | Cosmetic bags | Keyrings | Scarves |
| Cards | Curtain tie-backs | Lingerie bags | Scissors sheaths |
| Chatelaines | Cushions | Needlecases | Workbags |
| Clothing | Frames | Pictures | |

Many of these items are illustrated in this book and in *Ribbon Embroidery, Creative Ribbon Embroidery* and *The Complete Book of Ribbon Embroidery*, also by Heather Joynes and published by Kangaroo Press.